DISCOVERING CANADA

The Fur Traders

ROBERT LIVESEY & A.G. SMITH

First published in 1989 by
Stoddart Publishing Co. Limited
34 Lesmill Road
Toronto, Canada
M3B 2T6

CANADIAN CATALOGUING IN PUBLICATION DATA

Livesey, Robert, 1940-
  The Fur Traders

Includes index.
(Discovering Canada series)
ISBN 0-7737-5304-4

1. Fur Trade - Canada - History - Juvenile literature. 2. Canada - Exploring expeditions - Juvenile literature.3. Northwest, Canadian - Discovery and exploration - Juvenile literature. I. Smith, A.G. (Albert Gray), 1945-   . II. Title. III. Series.

FC3207. L58 1989   971   C89-094392-3
F1060.7. L58 1989

TEXT ILLUSTRATIONS: A.G. Smith

COVER ILLUSTRATION: Wes Lowe

COVER DESIGN: Brant Cowie/ ArtPlus Limited

TYPE OUTPUT: Tony Gordon Ltd.

Printed in Canada

To Alex and Nancy, with love

A special thanks to 'trapper' Rob Little, Josie Hazen, Susan Johnston, Michele Bonifacio, Greg Miller, David Densmore, Sandra Tooze, and the librarians at the Oakville Public Library, the Sheridan College Library and the University of Windsor Library for their help in producing this book.

Table of Contents

Introduction

A New World

 Imagine you are in a strange land stretching endlessly in front of you. The country is populated with hundreds of independent, native tribes that guard their territories against outsiders. There are no roads on which to travel through the thick forests, only rivers. On the other side of the mysterious continent, thousands of kilometres away, is the Pacific Ocean.

When Europeans first established settlements on the east coast of North America (first in Vinland, then New France, and later the New England colonies), they had no idea of the size or shape of this vast continent. They were sitting on the edge of a new world that was waiting to be discovered. There was curiosity to search for the "Western Sea," but something else caused the early explorers to risk their lives in the dangerous wilderness.

The main cause for the exploration of the country of Canada was an innocent and industrious little animal called the beaver. Back in Europe, the fur of the beaver was in great demand to make stylish hats. As the beaver population disappeared in the east, the white men were forced to push farther to the west and the north to meet the demand for beaver pelts.

The harmless little beaver unwittingly brought about the destruction of Indian cultures across the continent, the bloodshed of thousands of whites and natives, and the exploration of the North American continent. It should be no surprise to see the beaver on the back of every Canadian nickel and to know that it has become a national symbol of our country.

CHAPTER 1 *The Hunted*

The Beaver

Before the arrival of the white men from Europe, there were about ten million beaver living in North America. The beaver families did not like to travel or migrate; they preferred to live in one neighbourhood.

An adult beaver weighs between 14 and 28 kgs (30-60 lbs.). It lives with only one mate and the babies, called *cubs*, are born in May. Usually a mother gives birth to between two and six cubs at a time. The young cubs live on the milk of the mother for only six weeks, but live close to the mother in the family home or *lodge* for one year. Within 48 hours of his birth, a beaver cub is given his first swimming lesson by his father. They usually are full grown at two and a half years and find a mate of their own. An average beaver lodge has about nine family members of varying ages.

The beaver's food is wood and it is stored under water for the winter, at short distances from the lodge. A winter supply of food is mainly birch, cottonwood, poplar, willow and the bark or twigs of hardwoods. In the summer they enjoy the roots of various water plants.

Unlike squirrels, groundhogs, or bears, beavers do not hibernate and thus adapt to the cold northern climate by growing thick fur coats. Beavers who live in the far northwest have thicker, darker, more beautiful coats than their cousins in the south. A young beaver cub with soft black fur on its back (*guard hair* up to five cm [two in.] long) and lighter shorter fur on its stomach (*underhair* less than three cm [one in.] long) was the most valuable to the hunters. If you look at a beaver's hair through a microscope, you will see many small barbs. It was these barbs that made the fur so special for the manufacture of hats.

As the white men encouraged the natives to bring them more and more furs, the beaver communities were destroyed. This forced the fur traders to travel farther north and west in search of new and richer supplies of beaver pelts. Not only the beaver, but all fur-bearing animals became targets and many, such as the buffalo, became endangered species.

Beaver Lodges

The beavers are great construction workers. First, they build dams across streams to ensure a supply of water. Next they build lodges six metres (20 ft.) wide and one to two metres (three to five ft.) high. The thick walls are made of sticks, branches and small flat stones cemented together with mud.

Inside the beaver lodge is a circular chamber about half a metre (two ft.) high and two metres (six ft.) across. The floor of the chamber is about ten cm (four in.) above the water level. One metre (three ft.) below the water there are two secret, underwater entrances from two to three metres (five to ten ft.) long and about half-a-metre (two ft.) wide leading to the central chamber. One is used as a normal entrance; the other is used to carry in supplies of food. In addition to the lodge, the beaver has rooms or burrows along the banks of the river which also have underwater entrances.

Destruction of the Beaver

In his journal, the famous explorer, David Thompson, described the reason for the disappearance of the beaver.

Formerly the Beavers were very numerous, the many Lakes and Rivers gave them ample space, and the poor Indian had only a pointed stick sharpened and hardened in the fire, a stone Hatchet, Spear and Arrowheads of the same; thus armed he was weak against the sagacious Beaver who on the banks of a Lake made itself a house of a foot thick or more;... But when the arrival of the White People had changed all their weapons from stone to iron and steel and added the fatal Gun, every animal fell before the Indian...Thus armed the houses of the Beavers were pierced through, the Dams cut through, and the water of the Ponds lowered, or wholly run off, and the houses of the Beaver and their Burrows laid dry, by which means they became an easy prey to the Hunter.

Danger

The beaver's flat tail is used as a warning signal; with it he makes a loud slap on the water's surface to alert the others of danger.

Otter

2 *The Hunters*

Fur Traders

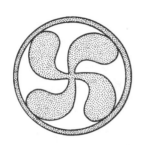 If your family decided to take a trip to a place that you had never visited before, most likely you would first obtain a map of the area, city, province, state, country, etc. The early fur hunters had no maps and the only roads through the thick wilderness were the dangerous rivers and lakes. These adventurous hunters who travelled into the unknown territories in search of furs came from a variety of backgrounds.

The first whites to explore the new continent befriended the native people, the Indians of North America, who taught them how to survive in the wilderness. The Indians also knew the river routes and forest paths that led to the vast interior of the North American continent.

The first whites who dared to explore the mysterious depths of the forests were young Frenchmen, the *coureurs de bois*, or "runners of the wood." These fearless adventurers, dressed in buckskins, were independent frontiersmen, hunting and trading furs to make a living in the hostile wilderness.

The European demand for beaver hats turned the fur trade into an industry. When the English established colonies to the south of the French, the competition for the fur trade became fierce. The Iroquois joined forces with the traders in the New England colonies, while the Hurons sided with the settlers of New France. This resulted in trade wars that led to the near extermination of the Hurons in 1649 and 1650.

When the English defeated the French on the Plains of Abraham in 1759, Montreal was overrun by an adventurous group of mainly Scottish and English merchants who were ambitious to take control of the rich fur trade. These merchant-traders created their own companies, hired the experienced French *voyageurs* who already knew the fur routes and began a ruthless rivalry over the pelts of the beaver and other animals. The competition led to fights and murders until, in 1779, the independent traders agreed to form one large company, the North West Company, in which they all had shares.

A new rivalry then began between the old Hudson's Bay Company, established in 1670, and the new, enterprising North West Company. Again it led to bloodshed and death, until the two companies merged in 1821.

Over the centuries, the fur traders of the northwest spent as much energy trying to destroy one another as they did trapping furs.

Partners of the North West Company belonged to a private association called the Beaver Club which had the special medallion shown above.

Vocabulary of the Fur Traders

French was the traditional language of the fur trade.

Voyageurs (Travellers)
These experienced French-Canadian canoe men whose hard labour moved the heavy loads across the continent paddled 14 to 16 hours a day. They were proud of their strength and ability to endure hardships. Their colourful caps and hand-woven sashes became the uniform of the fur trade. As a hockey player today values his stick, they had their own personal paddles which they painted in multi-coloured designs. They had no hope of ever becoming a partner or even a clerk in the company, and the hard work forced them to retire by the age of 40. A *voyageur* dreamed of shooting white rapids, surviving in the wilderness, and being known for his strength.

Portages (Carrying Places)

Along the canoe routes, the fur traders would have to switch from one river or lake to another, and avoid dangerous rapids and waterfalls. This meant they had to carry their canoes, supplies and loads for many miles on their backs. The heavy backpacks were held by leather straps around their foreheads. The strong-backed *voyageurs* used to carry two or three 40-kg (90-lb.) packs at the same time over a portage and then go back for another load. In total, about 3629 kgs (three tons) of cargo and canoes had to be portaged and there were 36 portages between Montreal and Georgian Bay.

Décharges   (Half-Portages)
If the swift-flowing rivers and rapids made it possible, the _voyageurs_ would avoid a portage. Part of the cargo would be left in the canoes while they were pulled along the shore with ropes.

Brigade (Convoy of Canoes)
When transporting furs or supplies the traders travelled in large convoys. Sometimes a brigade would include three hundred canoes.

Bourgeois   (Merchant-Traders)
These were the bosses. Their place in the canoe was just behind the middle seat but they did not paddle. They were usually partners in the fur trading company, and its flag would flap proudly on the prow of the _bourgeois'_ canoe. To control the Indians, clerks and _voyageurs_, they had to be good leaders. Because they were the only law and order on the rough trail or in a remote settlement, they had to make decisions on the spot.

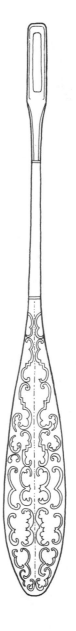

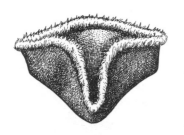

Military beaver hats

LaVieille (The Old Lady)
This was what the *voyageurs* called the wind. When they came to Lake Huron's Georgian Bay where sudden storms could destroy a canoe, the superstitious *voyageurs* would throw trinkets and bits of tobacco into the water as a gift to "the old lady" so that she would not cause them trouble.

Pays d'en Haut (High-Country)
This was the name given to the far northwest territories beyond Grand Portage, the *entrepôt*.

Entrepôt (Warehouse)
The point where the Montreal Canoes met with the North Canoes and exchanged cargoes of trading goods for cargoes of furs was Grand Portage (or in later years, after 1803, Fort William). The turn-around point, or *entrepôt*, was necessary because the longer Montreal Canoes could not navigate on the narrower, faster rivers of the far northwest, just as the North Canoes were too small to survive the high waves and sudden storms of the Great Lakes.

Civilian beaver hats

Métis (Half Indian-Half White)
Many white-skinned explorers
married native women and thus
this mixed race of people came to
exist in the northwest.

Hommes du Nord (Northmen)
Only a few hundred men from the
legendary days of the fur trade
could brag that they were northmen. It was a highly honoured title
and involved an initiation ceremony in which the new comer was
drenched with water and made to
swear an oath.

Mangeurs de Lard (Pork Eaters)
Voyageurs on the Montreal route
ate dried peas or beans, sea biscuits
and salt pork. This was considered
a luxurious diet by the tough men
of the north who used to call them
mangeurs de lard, or "pork eaters."

Maize Mush and Bear Grease
Around Lake Huron the food was
maize mush, which was an Indian
corn, mixed with bacon fat or bear
grease.

13

Pemmican (Buffalo Meat)
The main food in western areas from Rainy Lake to the Rockies was pemmican, which was sun-dried, pounded buffalo meat with melted tallow poured over it. For an extra treat Saskatoon berries would sometimes be mixed into it. Pemmican was very concentrated, highly nutritious and lasted for months. The *voyageurs* carried it in 40-kg (90-lb.) containers made from animal hides.

Pot au Beurre (Butter Tub)
This was the jail at Grand Portage where *voyageurs* were put to sober up and cool off when they got into fights. A creek divided the rows of upturned Montreal Canoes, under which the "pork eaters" slept, from the hundreds of weather-beaten tents of the northmen. Fist fights erupted constantly as the *hommes du nord* and *mangeurs de lard* threw insults at one another to prove who was stronger.

The Poetic Frontiersman

Henry Kelsey, working for the Hudson's Bay Company, was the first white man to reach the western plains and the first to see a buffalo. Kelsey's journals have puzzled historians for years because, rather than expressing his experiences clearly, he liked to write in poetry. For example, he writes about the route he took to The Pas, Manitoba in 1690:

Distance from hence by judgement at ye lest
From ye House (Y.F.) 600 miles southwest
Through rivers which run strong with falls
Thirty-three carriages, five lakes in all.

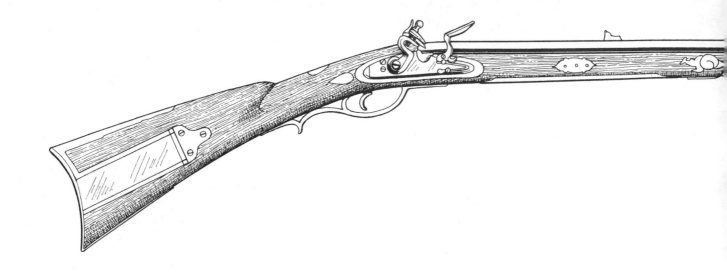

Native Partners

The canoe routes used by the *voyageurs* had been established by the native people since the last ice age. In the wilderness economy of the fur-trading industry, the Indians were trading partners and thus friendly relationships based on trust and equality were developed. The fur-trading companies were the only law and order that existed and their good relationship with the natives who supplied them with furs was a type of partnership.

In contrast, was the "wild west" of the American frontier, where the white intruders were settlers who regarded the Indians as an enemy who had to be pushed off the land. American law and order was white-man's law, with elected sheriffs or marshals who seldom represented the natives.

Write a Movie Script

What You Need:
a pen or pencil and some paper **or** a microcomputer with a word-processing kit

What To Do:

1. Invent a cast and plot, such as:
   - a *homme du nord* encounters a *mangeur de lard*.
   - an old Indian woman or man gives advice to a youngster.
   - a *voyageur* befriends an Indian.
   - two Métis women talk about a handsome young *bourgeois*.

2. Create a conversation:
   - each character should have a unique personality and name.
   - use as many words as possible from the *voyageur's* vocabulary.
   - create a conflict between the viewpoints of the characters.
   - the emotions and actions of the people should become stronger and stronger, until they reach a climax (a physical response, a decision, an agreement, etc.).

3. Use costumes and props. Dress as the people; use makeup, canoe paddles or toy weapons.

4. Act out your script. Practise with a friend or family member. If you have a camera, film it.

18

CHAPTER 3 *Women of the Fur Trade*

Natives and Métis

The Indian and Métis women of the northwest seldom received fame or honour. Their names did not become known in the history books, but they were as strong willed and hard working as the men.

The fur traders depended on these women for food. The women would dress the game, cut the meat into strips and place it on a rack to dry in the sun or over a fire. Using wooden-handled stone mallets and a hollow log, they pounded the dried buffalo meat into pemmican. The pounding, like a war drum, could be heard for miles across the prairies and through the forests. They would then place 22 kgs (50 lbs.) of lean meat into a buffalo-hide bag and pour 18 kgs (40 lbs.) of melted fat on top to seal it. Finally they would load the 40-kg (90-lb.) lots of pemmican into canoes.

Voyageurs would also depend on the women to keep their canoes in working condition. They were the "pit mechanics." At every stop women would examine each bark canoe, mending the rips and tears with *watope* prepared from cedar roots and sealing the repair with tree gum. They had to gather the *watope* and gum in the forests and prepare it.

The women also made the clothing. They netted the snowshoes, sewed the buckskin jackets and pants and made the men's moccasins. In addition, if there were no horse or dog-drawn *travois*, the women would haul the heavy bundles themselves. Indian men refused to do such work because a warrior would lose face if he stooped to carry a load.

Many of the fur traders took Indian wives or girlfriends for company on the trail. Most left their women and children behind in the northwest when they quit the trade and returned to white civilization. However, it was not a one-sided relationship. The young women were excited to be the partner of a rich and romantic adventurer, and frequently the marriage of a fur trader to the daughter of a chief was part of a business agreement. The Indian tribe gained an important member of the family who had access to the trading goods from the east, and the trader was certain his new in-laws would not trade valuable furs to a rival company.

The marriage ceremony in the northwest was a simple one, *au façon du nord* (in the way of the north). The man would offer a gift of a blanket, a gun, or a horse, to the father of the bride. If the gift was accepted, the marriage was complete.

Young Brides

In the days of the fur traders, girls married at a young age, as soon as they were capable of having babies. For example, the famous frontiersman, Pierre LaVérendrye, at 21, became engaged to Marie-Anne Dandonneau, when she was only 12 years old.

True Love

One young trader, Daniel Harmon, who was from a strict New England family, bragged that he would never marry a native. However, when a chief offered him his 14-year-old daughter, Daniel could not resist her beauty. At first he planned to leave her behind when he retired from the fur trade, but 19 years later he was still in love and could not part from her. He took her and their children back to his home in New England.

The Woman Who Wouldn't Leave

After a New Year's Eve party at one of the prairie posts, Alexander Henry, the Younger, brought an Indian woman to his house. The next day he tried to get her to return home, but she refused to go. He left on a buffalo hunt, but when he returned many days later she was still in his house. Nothing could convince her to return to her tribe. Alexander wrote in his journal: "The devil couldn't have got rid of her." She became his wife and they remained happily married.

Love at First Sight

While passing through the trading post at Ile à la Crosse in the summer of 1799, David Thompson saw Charlotte Small, a half-Irish, half-Cree girl of 14 with long black hair. He fell in love at first sight and married her immediately. She became his faithful companion on his exploits into the unknown Rockies. David remained with his family, which grew to 16 children.

Indian women enjoyed making birch-bark patterns which they used for bead work.

Make a Birch Bark Basket

Indians made baskets and other containers from the bark of birch trees. Using the cut-out on page 23, follow the instructions carefully to make your own birch bark basket.

What You Need:
scissors
white glue

What To Do:
1. Cut out the large "bark" shape.

2. Apply glue to one tab marked with a dot (.). Bring up the opposite side and press it to the tab (do not apply too much glue or it will seep out and spoil the surface). Repeat this process on the other three corners. Your basket is now complete and ready for picking berries.

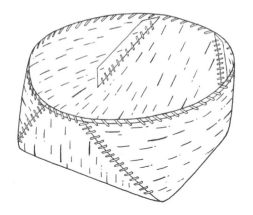

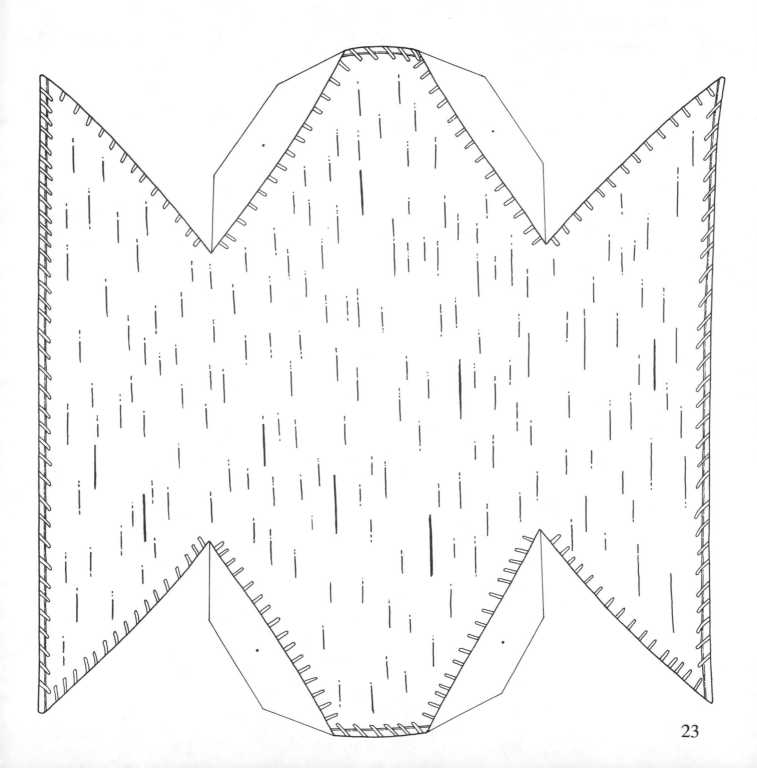

23

Cut out from the other side

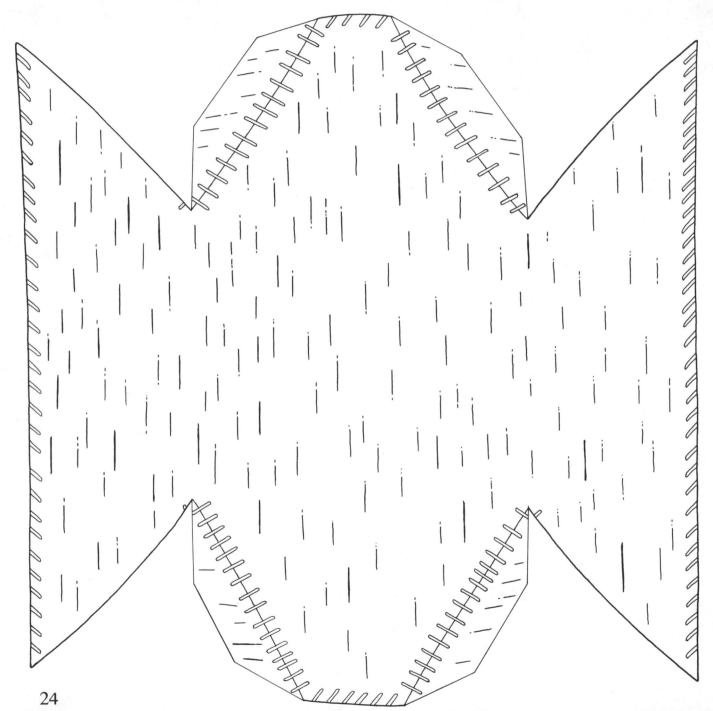

4 *The Bay To The North*

Pierre Radisson

When you go out to play with your friends, your mother or father probably says, "Don't go too far!" or "Be careful!" or "Watch out for strangers!"

When 16-year-old Pierre and his two young friends decided to go hunting in the woods outside the settlement of Trois Rivières in 1651, their parents most likely gave them some kind of warning. Pierre Radisson had just come from France that year, and the wild beauty of the thick, Canadian forests surrounding his new home looked inviting.

Without warning, a band of tall Iroquois warriors pounced on the startled boys. The three youths stood terrorized and shuddering as their clothing was ripped off their bodies, and they were subjected to torture as they were dragged back to the Iroquois camp.

Later, Pierre looked down the long corridor of eager, screaming warriors violently waving wooden clubs and saw their purpose at once. He would have to run between the two lines while they tried to club his already exhausted body. To them it was a game; to him it meant death.

Determined not to show fear, he sprang forward, dashing, jumping, weaving, shoving his way through. Amazingly, he reached the other end. Probably it was his speed and bravery that impressed one of the Iroquois chiefs to such an extent that he adopted the white boy. Pierre's two companions were not so lucky; they were killed.

For the next two years Pierre lived with the Indians — adopted their

customs, dressed like them, even stained his body as they did. But finally he managed to escape and, in March of 1654, returned to Trois Rivières. His ordeal as a captive had taught him the ways of the woods. He was now a *coureur de bois* and set out on a fur-trading expedition.

By 1660, Pierre had gone into partnership with his brother-in-law, des Groseilliers, and they planned a hazardous journey to the unexplored northwest to seek furs. They asked the governor for a licence, but he refused. They set out without his permission, travelling to the Lake Superior region and beyond. With the help of friendly Cree and Sioux Indians, they returned to Montreal with 300 canoes overflowing with valuable furs. But the governor took 90 percent of their load as a penalty for trading without a licence.

Furious and frustrated, Radisson and des Groseilliers slipped secretly out of the colony in 1661, and pushed farther into the northwest. There they discovered "the bay to the north," which was really Hudson Bay.

With his quick imagination Pierre immediately saw the possibilities. Large sailing ships could travel from Europe directly to the shores of Hudson Bay and return with far more furs than he could carry in small canoes. It would save the long trips up angry rivers and through hostile forests. But the French officials, who financed large vessels, laughed at his crazy scheme.

So, Pierre travelled to England where Prince Rupert gave him two ships, the *Eaglet* and the *Nonsuch*. When the first shipload of furs arrived in England, the king granted Prince Rupert a charter to trade in the northwest. It became known as Rupert's Land and Pierre's vision became a reality with the formation of the Hudson's Bay Company.

Pierre Radisson, one of the bravest of the *coureurs de bois*, the man who opened "the bay to the north," died in England in 1710.

Torture or Test ?

The Iroquois lived a rough and rugged life, and in their culture a boy was worthy of being a warrior only if he could survive torture without showing weakness. Today, a Canadian youngster is tested when he or she rushes the length of a hockey rink or lacrosse field, enduring body checks and slashing sticks.

Canoes of the Fur Traders

In frontier days the roads were the rivers and lakes. Today trucks, trains and airplanes carry cargoes across the continent; in early days the primary transportation vehicle was the canoe.

Canot de Nord (North Canoe)

The smaller North Canoe was eight metres (25 ft.) long, over one m (four ft.) wide and carried a crew of four to eight men. It could carry only half the cargo of a Montreal Canoe, about 1500 kgs (a ton and a half). A good *voyageur* paddled 40 strokes a minute from dawn to dusk. It was a common sport for canoes to race across Lake Winnipeg, and then they would aver-

age as many as 60 strokes a minute. On one occasion two crews raced for 40 hours before a *bourgeois* ordered them to stop.

Canot de Maître (Montreal Canoe)
The Montreal Canoe was a larger vessel, about 11 metres (36 ft.) in length, about two metres (six ft.) wide and able to carry 3000 kgs (three tons) plus a crew of six to 12. Although it had no metal in its construction, it could survive the stormy waves of the Great Lakes or the deadly rapids of the Ottawa River. However, this giant canoe was too large to travel the smaller rivers between Lake Superior and Lake Athabasca.

Express Canoe

When the fur companies had urgent news or messages, such as special mail or orders, a shift in the market, the beginning or end of a war, etc., that had to reach their wilderness forts, they would use as many as 14 men in a Montreal Canoe or nine in a North Canoe to ensure speed rather than capacity. It was the highest honour for a proud *voyageur* to be chosen to paddle an express canoe. Six northmen once took Roderick McKenzie a distance of 3200 km (2000 mi.) from Rainy Lake to Fort Chipewyan in a month and four days.

York Boats

In 1774, Samuel Hearne established Cumberland House as the Hudson's Bay Company's first major inland post. Via the Saskatchewan River, it was connected to the Rocky Mountains and Lake Winnipeg.

Beginning in 1797, the Hudson's Bay Company used York Boats along the mainline route from York to Edmonton and on the larger prairie rivers west of Lake Winnipeg, whereas the North West Company used North Canoes. The York Boat had a pointed bow and stern and was a little larger than a Montreal Canoe. It had about the same capacity for freight as a Montreal Canoe, but needed only a small crew of six to nine *Orkneymen*, and thus did not need the skilled paddling talents of *voyageurs*. The York Boat was more durable and could be operated at a 33 percent savings over a freight canoe. Because of its great weight it had to be dragged or winched on rollers over portages; this eliminated its use on the smaller and rockier rivers north of the Saskatchewan River.

The *Nonsuch*

FUR TRADING FORT
ON
HUDSON BAY
C. 1775

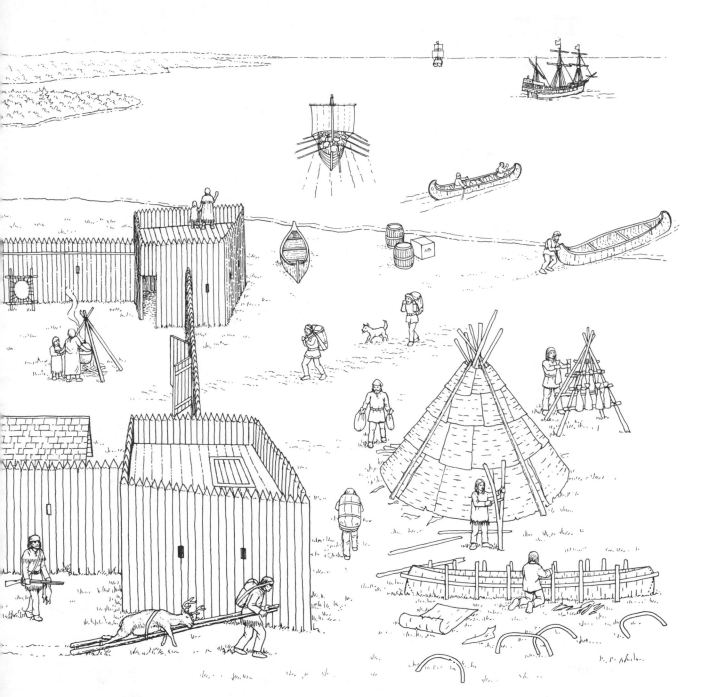

Make a Birch Bark Canoe

Birch bark contains oil that makes it very water resistant. Many Indian tribes used birch bark to make canoes. Using the cut-outs on page 35, follow the instructions to build your own paper model.

What You Need:
scissors
white glue
coloured pencils or crayons
scoring tool

What To Do:

1. Colour the pieces of the canoe before cutting it out. Do not colour the glue tabs. Suggestion:
   - inside of canoe and thwarts (cross pieces) - light brown
   - paddles - light brown with red or yellow tips
   - outside of canoe colour the gunwales (wooden edge around the sides) - light brown
   - leave the birch bark white

2. Cut out the hull piece. Score lightly along the edges of the bow and stern. Apply glue along the inside edges of the stem and stern and press them carefully together.

3. After the ends have dried, apply glue to the four seam tabs, one at a time, and press them together.

4. Fold the thwarts and glue them together. After they have dried, cut them out and glue them in position — the straight one in the centre and the angled ones near the ends.

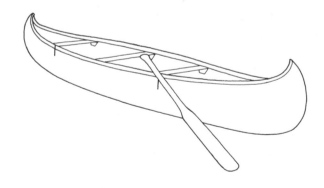

5. Fold the paddles and glue them together. After they have dried cut them out and lay them inside the canoe.

If you would like to actually try your canoe in water, you may waterproof it a bit by applying a thin coating of vegetable oil to the outside.

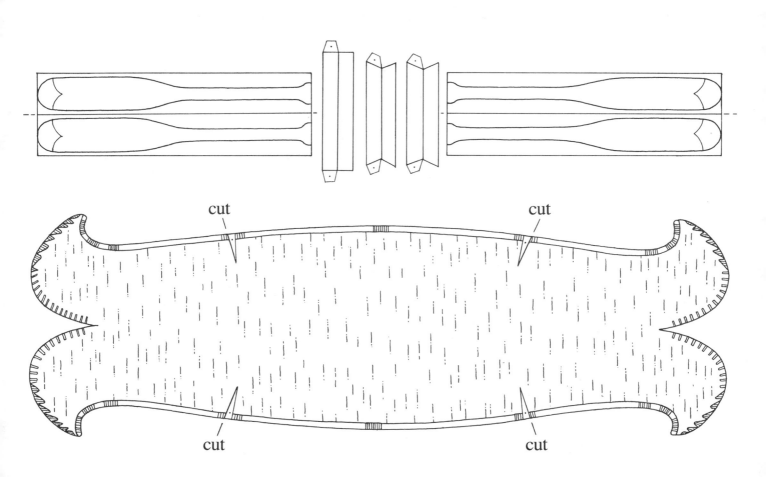

cut   cut

cut   cut

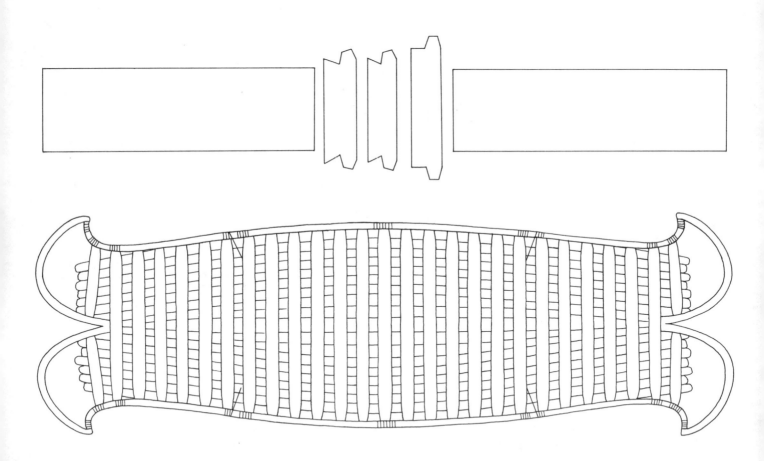

CHAPTER 5 *West to the Rockies*

The LaVérendryes

All people have goals in their lives — dreams that they hope to accomplish. Some, like Pierre LaVérendrye, devote their entire lives to a specific task, but fail to complete it. As you know from playing sports, everyone cannot win. However, it is a reward to know that you tried your best and enjoyed the adventure.

LaVérendrye was the first of the fur-trading explorers to be born in Canada. At the age of 12, Pierre became a naval cadet and studied military drills, camping techniques, arithmetic, map making, surveying, record keeping, and first aid. As a teenager, he was always listening to the tales told by *coureurs de bois* of *le pays d'en haut* (the northwest), and *la mer de l'ouest* (the Western Sea). He became a fur trader and his first command was Fort Ste. Anne at Nipigon on the tip of Lake Superior. Pierre and his wife, Marie-Anne, had six children; four were boys. As they grew older, his teenage sons joined him in the fur trade.

Although he worked in the fur trade for the money, LaVérendrye's real dream was to explore, to reach the Western Sea and discover a new route to China. The Indians who brought furs to his fort told him about an unusual Indian tribe to the west called the Mandans, who lived in houses rather than tepees, grew garden crops rather than hunted, and had white skins. He set out to find the mysterious tribe.

When he and two of his sons reached the Mandan villages, LaVérendrye was disappointed. They did not live close to the Western Sea; instead, there

was an endless sea of flat prairies. He returned to his fort, leaving his sons, François and Louis-Joseph, to continue the search.

On April 29, 1742, the two sons continued westward. By late July they crossed the Missouri River and headed southwest. Their Mandan guides refused to go farther, but they met a party of Crow Indians. The Crows didn't know about a Western Sea, but took them to another tribe. And so they continued west, from tribe to tribe, until they came to the Horse

Indians. This tribe was under attack from the Shoshoni, who were destroying their villages and taking their women and children as slaves.

The LaVérendryes could not persuade the Horse Indians to go westward into Shoshoni territory, but another tribe, the Bow Indians (a branch of the Pawnees) invited the Frenchmen to join their war party against the Shoshoni. Since it would get them farther west, they agreed.

They joined over 2000 proud warriors who rode bareback on powerful horses, wore war paint and carried shields of buffalo hide. Behind them followed crowds of women and children, as well as packs of half-wild dogs dragging *travois*.

On New Year's Day, 1743, the LaVérendrye brothers became the first white men to see the Rocky Mountains, actually the Bighorn Mountains of Wyoming. They were certain that once they crossed the mountains, they would find the Western Sea.

Mandan Indians performing a buffalo dance (after George Catlind).

But fate was against them. The Bow Indians had left their women and children a few days behind for safety. When the men arrived at the Shoshoni camp it was deserted. In panic they imagined the Shoshoni had slipped around them and were attacking the defenceless women and children. They rushed back to their camp. It was a false alarm; their people were safe. Nevertheless, the Bows decided to return to their own territory, and the LaVérendryes were forced to stay with their protectors. Sadly, they retreated, leaving the Rocky Mountains behind. Although they came close, the LaVérendryes failed to reach the Western Sea.

Pierre LaVérendrye suddenly became ill and died in Montreal on December 5, 1749 at age 64. At the time he was planning a new trip to the western Rockies via the Saskatchewan River. Six years after his death, Anthony Henday of the Hudson's Bay Company made the trip and became the first explorer to see the Canadian Rockies.

Historic Discovery

When LaVérendrye sent his two sons, François and Louis-Joseph, westward, he gave them a lead plaque with a message engraved in Latin:

In the 26th year of the reign of Louis XV by the grace of God most illustrious ruler. By the grace of God Marquis de Beauharnois, 1741. Placed by Pierre Gaultier de la Vérendrye.

The sons buried it on March 30, 1743. In 1913, some school children found it near the town of Pierre, South Dakota.

Astrolabe

When François and Louis-Joseph LaVérendrye made their journey to the Rocky Mountains, they carried an astrolabe. This primitive instrument of the sixteenth century allowed them to determine their geographic position.

Make an Indian Tepee

The Indians of the great Plains made their tepees of buffalo hides that were sewn together and stretched over poles. Using the cut-outs on page 43, follow the instructions to make your own tepee.

What You Need:
scissors
white glue
coloured pencils or crayons
a scoring tool

What To Do:

1. Colour the geometric design using bright colours.
   Do not colour the glue tabs.

2. Cut out the tepee.

3. Score along the fold line of the vent flaps and fold them back.

4. Apply glue to the tabs above and below the doorway. Bring them around and under the opposite edge and press the pieces together. Allow the glue to dry.

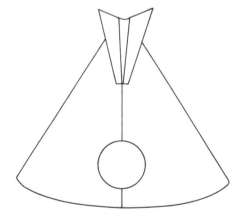

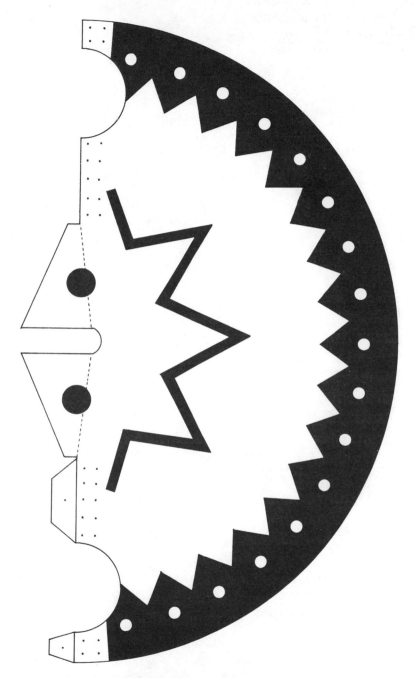

Using this design, you and your friends could make a village of tepees.

43

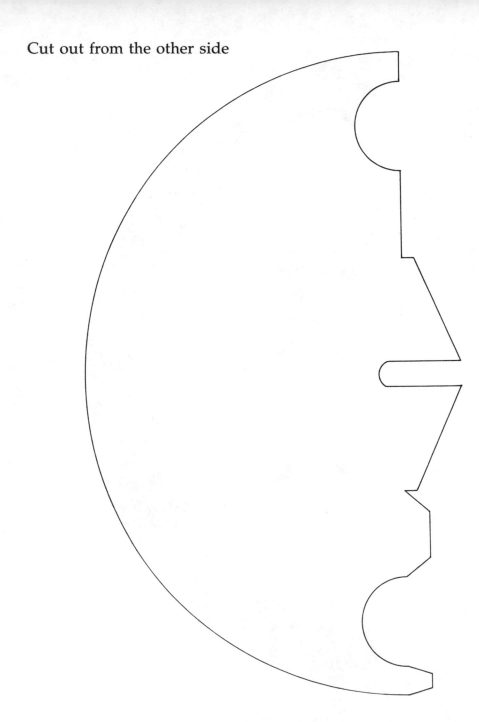

6 First Across The Continent

Alexander Mackenzie

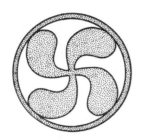

Canada is the second-largest country in the world. It stretches from the Atlantic Ocean to the Pacific Ocean. Our unique geography challenges us to conquer it.

There is always some Canadian setting out on a quest to cross the continent from coast to coast. One day it may be you. Some walk, run, hitchhike or pedal a bike. Others drive motorcycles, cars, campers or trucks. There are those who prefer trains, airplanes, hot-air balloons or covered wagons. Terry Fox and Rick Hanson attempted it for charity.

The first person to cross the North American continent was a young Scottish fur trader, Alexander Mackenzie. No one had found a passage through the Rocky Mountains to the Pacific Ocean when he set out in 1792 determined to try. His eight-metre-long (26 ft.) birch-bark canoe held six *voyageurs*, two Indian hunters and his second-in-command, Alexander Mackay. By mid-May they had reached the dangerous, swirling vortex of the Peace River Canyon, where the canoe could no longer be paddled.

As Mackenzie's group proceeded slowly up the Parsnip River, a hunting party of Sekanis Indians sprang from the forest, bows taut and arrows quivering. Mackenzie ordered his men not to touch their guns and, with glass beads and trinkets, he won the natives' friendship. They told him that a river to the south led to the "stinking lake" (Pacific Ocean).

As they climbed higher, the Parsnip shrank to a maze of small streams. On June 12, 1792 they became the first white people to cross the Continental Divide. Now they started downstream looking for a river that would

take them to the ocean. Rapids smashed the canoe on a rock. Almost all their ammunition was lost. Soaked and mutinous, the men demanded they return home; however, Mackenzie shamed them into continuing by talking about the "disgrace" of failure.

On June 18, when they reached what would later be known as the Fraser River, a shower of arrows sprayed them from the river bank. Again, Mackenzie ordered his men not to shoot, and stepped ashore alone. This time it was the war-like Carrier Indians, but he gave them gifts and the chief told him of a safer river to the west.

After two weeks of struggling with 40-kg (90-lb.) packs across hard-packed snow trails, they descended into the Bella Coola River Valley. There, a friendly chief loaned them two dugout canoes and a crew that took them down to a coastal inlet. The water tasted salty! They were almost there. But the Indians refused to go on.

From another Indian village, they obtained a clumsy, leaking canoe that took them to what is now Dean Channel. Suddenly, they were attacked by three canoes of Indians from the Bella Bella nation. The chief claimed that other white men in "giant canoes at sea" had already been there and a white chief named Macubah (Vancouver) had shot at him. Now he wanted

revenge. When ten more canoes loaded with natives arrived, Mackenzie and his men primed their weapons for a fight. But instead of attacking, the Indians mysteriously withdrew.

The next morning Mackenzie wrote:

I now mixed up some vermillion in melted grease and wrote in large letters, on the rock on which we had slept last night: Alexander Mackenzie, from Canada by land, the twenty-second of July, one thousand seven hundred and ninety-three.

Back To School

Mackenzie was determined to reach the Pacific, but he realized that he needed more than instinct and Indian legends to get there. So, he left the northwest wilderness, paddled back to Montreal, took a tall ship to England and studied navigation for a year and a half. When he returned in 1792, he had the knowledge and instruments to accomplish his dream.

River Disappointment

Mackenzie finally reached the Pacific Ocean in 1793, but it was not his first attempt. In 1789, along with 13 companions in three canoes, he followed an unknown river north for six weeks, over 2,400 km (4,000 mi.) but instead of turning west and emptying into the Pacific, the river took him to the Arctic Ocean. He called it "River Disappointment," but today it has been renamed the Mackenzie River in his honour.

The Lost Dog

When Alexander Mackenzie set out to search for the Western Sea in 1793, he was accompanied by his lieutenant Alexander Mackay, two Indians, six French-Canadian *voyageurs* and a dog. During a clash with a hostile tribe of natives, at what Mackenzie named Rascal's Village, the dog disappeared. Alexander was very upset when he recorded the loss of his pet in his journal. He proceeded to the Pacific Ocean, but on his return he had to pass by Rascal's Village again. In the midst of the thick forest he met his lost dog, who was frightened and thin from hunger. He welcomed the dog with scraps of food and the animal joined him for the trip back home.

White Water

The following description is from the diary of Alexander Mackenzie:
Monday May 20, 1793

Now with very much difficulty, we moved along at the bottom of a high rock. Luckily - it was not hard stone - we were able to cut steps in the rock for twenty feet. Then at the risk of my own life, I leaped onto a small rock below. There, I received upon my shoulders those who followed me along the steps. In this way the four of us passed the rock. Then we dragged up the canoe, but in doing so we broke it upon the rocks in the water.

As we went on the current ran faster and faster. In a distance of two miles, we had to unload the canoe four times and carry everything.

At five o'clock, we arrived at a point where the river was one continual rapid...the water was so rough that a wave striking the canoe broke the towing line. It seemed that the canoe would be broken to pieces, and those in her would be killed. And then another wave drove the boat out of the tumbling water. At last the men could bring the canoe ashore.

For as far as we could see, the river ahead of us was one white sheet of foaming water.

Keep a Journal

We know about the lives of the early fur traders because they kept journals. Try keeping a journal of your life for the next week. The most interesting thing about a journal is reading it a year later and realizing how your opinions and life have changed.

What You Need:
a pencil or pen
a small notebook

What To Do:
1. The fur trader's journal was a record of the daily events in his life. Record the things you do throughout the day.
For example:
"July 18, 1990: Woke up at 7:30.
Rode my bike to Jim's house. Jason, Carol and Diane were there. We rode our bikes around town."

2. Explorers made detailed descriptions of the environment so that they could later draw a map or tell a friend.
For example:
"The creek at the west side of town was much wider than usual due to the heavy rain last night. The water looked dangerous."

3. The fur traders were businessmen and thus recorded the number of furs they obtained and the trade goods they exchanged for them. Your journal can show how you spend your money:
"We stopped at the mall; I bought a pair of sunglasses for $5.95."

4. Fur traders also recorded personal conflicts and what they thought about them.
For example:
"Jason was acting strangely; he picked a fight with Diane. I think something is troubling him."

5. Sometimes a fur trader would record his private thoughts:
"Do they have shopping malls in China? What would an African kid my age be doing today? One day I want to travel around the world."

51

7 *Shooting the Rapids*

Simon Fraser

If you are in the position of choosing someone to work with, you want a person who you can depend upon and who will be loyal.

Simon Fraser was a dependable, loyal employee of the North West Company. He had been a *homme du nord* since age 16, travelling the northwest from Grand Portage to New Caledonia (now British Columbia).

Large sailing ships on the Pacific Ocean had reached the mouth of the Columbia River by sea and the North West Company was anxious to find a land route through the Rockies. In 1807, they sent orders to Simon Fraser to explore the Tacouche Tesse River down to the Pacific to discover if it might be the Columbia. This was a river Alexander Mackenzie had avoided because it was too violent to descend by canoe.

Without fear, Simon set out in four canoes with two lieutenants (Stuart and Quesnel), 19 *voyageurs* and two Indian guides. As the days passed, the river became more violent. It was insane to continue, but Fraser had been given a task and he took pride in finishing it.

They came to a three-kilometre-long (two-mile) gorge. High walls of rock rose on both sides of the narrow passage. Five *voyageurs* went first in a light canoe, but they lost control and were swirled about in the fast, foaming rapids, ricocheting off the rocky walls until they crashed on a projecting rock. In order to rescue them, the others cut steps in the cliff side and pulled the canoe, baggage and men up the perpendicular rock face, then portaged around the gorge.

But things got worse! On June 4, they came to a huge precipice blocking the entire river (Bar Rock). Below it was a series of rapids and whirlpools. It was impossible to portage so they had to shoot the rapids. Amazingly, they made it to the bottom, then returned by foot for their supplies. Inching his way along the rocky precipice with a heavy pack on his back, one man got stuck. He couldn't go forward or back. Fraser crawled on hands and knees to his rescue and cut the thongs of the back pack. It hurtled into the swirling waters below. Without the weight, the man crawled to safety.

Five days later Fraser couldn't believe his eyes. These rapids were even worse than the earlier ones! Again it was impossible to portage, so they had to brave the deadly white waters. He wrote in his diary:

...the water rolls down this extraordinary passage in tumultuous waves and with great velocity...skimming along as fast as lightening, the crews followed each other in awful silence, and when we arrived at the end, we stood gazing at each other in silent congratulation at our narrow escape from total destruction.

Their ordeal continued with day after day of frightening rapids and long painful portages. Their shoes were torn from their swollen, bleeding feet. At times they had to climb swinging, half-rotten rope ladders up the sheer sides of rock walls. They abandoned the canoes and with 36-kg (80-lb.) packs on their backs, set out to walk to the ocean.

Fraser and his men obtained new canoes from the Askettih Indians where the Thompson River flows into the Fraser. But more rapids blocked their way. At the mouth of the Coquihalla River, they sighted several seals. The ocean had to be close. They came to a deserted Misquiame Indian village where they were suddenly surprised by screaming warriors, dressed in "coats of mail" and swinging war clubs, but they escaped.

When Fraser finally calculated his latitude at the mouth of the river, it was 49° north latitude, not 46° 20'. This was not the Columbia. Disappointed, Fraser returned home. The river that he conquered bears his name to this day.

Rough Ride

One of Fraser's men who clung to an upturned canoe through five km (three mi.) of rapids and whirlpools described the experience:

I continued astride the canoe...I scarcely had time to look about me... In the second or third cascade the canoe plunged from a great height into an eddy below, and striking with great violence against the bottom, split in two. Here I lost my recollection...I soon recovered and was surprised to find myself on a smooth, easy current, with only one-half of the canoe in my arms.

1,200 Handshakes

When Simon Fraser arrived on June 19, 1807, at a village of the Haca-maugh, he was greeted by the chief who took him by the arm and led him into the village. Fraser wrote:
Here his people were sitting in rows to the number of twelve hundred, and I had to shake hands with the whole!

Smoking Gods

In 1805, when Fraser crossed the mountains by the Peace River Pass and paddled up the Nechaco River, he came into contact with an Indian tribe called the Carriers. When the astonished Carriers saw the white men with pipes blowing smoke from their mouths, they thought that they were superior beings gifted with supernatural powers.

Soap-Eating Indian

One of Fraser's men thought he would play a trick on a Carrier woman, so he offered her a piece of soap instead of meat. The joke backfired. She ate the soap but, despite the streams of soap suds flowing from her mouth, seemed to enjoy its unusual flavour.

Voyageur Adventure Game

On the following pages are the instructions, board and pieces needed to play an exciting game of adventure and trading.

What You Need:
2 to 4 players
1 die of a pair of dice
some paper
pencil
scissors

What To Do:

1. Before you begin to play, make 6 packs of supplies and 6 boxes of trade goods for each player using the patterns on page 60.

2. Also, make about 6 bundles of furs and 6 packs of supplies per player to be held in the "pot."

3. Cut out the adventure cards on page 61.

4. Read the playing rules on page 63.

5. Make or choose a counter that you can move along the board. It could be a favourite stone, a button or a bottle cap.

Voyageur

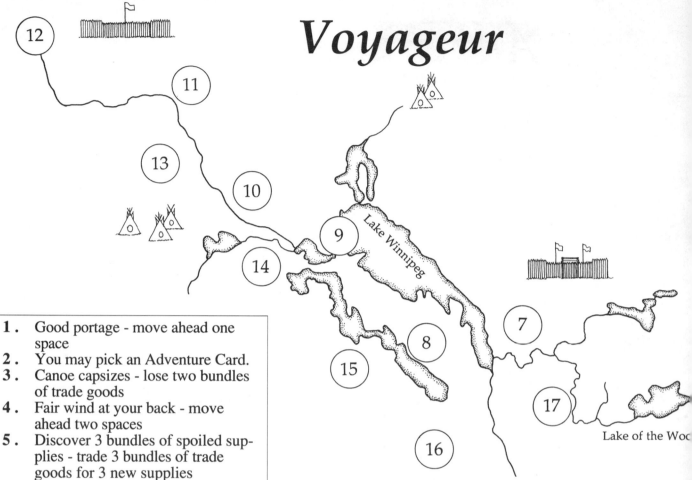

1. Good portage - move ahead one space
2. You may pick an Adventure Card.
3. Canoe capsizes - lose two bundles of trade goods
4. Fair wind at your back - move ahead two spaces
5. Discover 3 bundles of spoiled supplies - trade 3 bundles of trade goods for 3 new supplies
6. You may pick an Adventure Card.
7. Find shorter route around rapids - move ahead one space
8. Stop to repair canoe seams - turn in 1 extra bundle of supplies
9. Short of supplies - trade one bundle of trade goods for supplies
10. Canoe overturns - you are saved but lose all supplies. Return to Montreal and start over.
11. You may pick an Adventure Card.

12. You pass the halfway point: Trade each remaining bundle of trade goods with native people for a bundle of furs. Receive 6 bundles of new supplies from the pot.
13. Skirmish with rival traders - lose one turn
14. Swift current - move ahead one space
15. You may pick an Adventure Card.

Lake Winnipeg

Lake of the Woo

Adventure

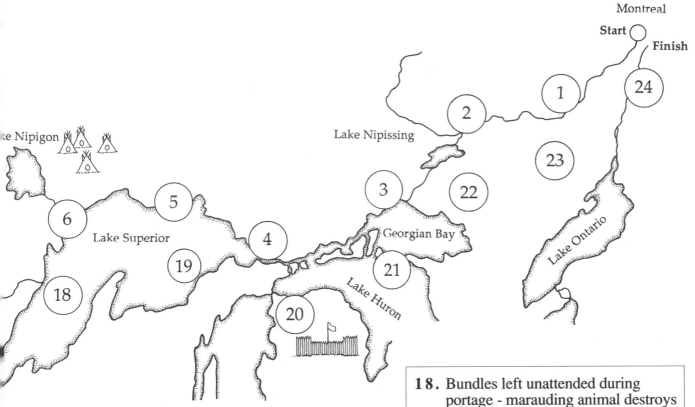

Montreal

Start

Finish

Lake Nipigon

Lake Nipissing

Lake Superior

Georgian Bay

Lake Huron

Lake Ontario

18. Bundles left unattended during portage - marauding animal destroys two bundles of supplies and one bundle of trade goods
19. You may pick an Adventure Card.
20. Canoe upset by fast moving submerged log - lose half your fur bundles
21. You may pick an Adventure Card.
22. Good progress - move ahead one turn
23. You may pick an Adventure Card.

16. One canoe missing - go back one space to check on it
17. Mysterious disease strikes most of your crew - turn in two bundles of supplies

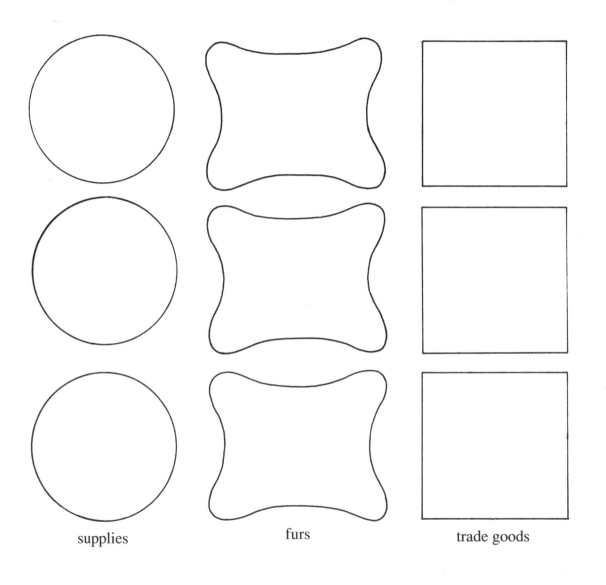

supplies   furs   trade goods

Trace or photocopy these patterns (see instructions on page 57).

Adventure Cards:

Snow blizzard - lose 2 bundles of supplies and 1 bundle of trade goods or furs. (into pot)

You have taken a wrong route - go back three spaces.

Indian attack - You save the lives of your rival traders. Each of the other players must give you 1 bundle of trade goods or furs.

Take a shorter route around rapids and gain 2 bundles of supplies. (from the pot)

You meet starving traders who are out of supplies - If you wish, you may trade them 1 bundle of supplies for 2 bundles of trade goods or furs. (from the pot)

While packing up camp after an overnight stop you discover some of your supplies missing - lose 2 bundles of supplies or 1 bundle of trade goods or furs. (into pot)

Fur trading fort has overstocked trade goods and trade you 2 bundles of trade goods for 1 bundle of supplies. (from the pot)

At a portage, friendly Indians ask for food. You trade 2 bundles of supplies for 4 bundles of furs. (from the pot)

Adventure Cards:

Adventure Card	Adventure Card
Adventure Card	Adventure Card
Adventure Card	Adventure Card
Adventure Card	Adventure Card

How To Play:

1. Each player begins with 6 packs of supplies and 6 boxes of trade goods.

2. The object of the game is to move safely along the route and barter your trade goods for furs. The player who returns to Montreal with 20 bundles of furs is the winner.

3. You may play through the game more than once. For longer games, set the goal of the game at 50 bundles, 100 bundles, etc.

4. Roll the die to see who moves first. The first player moves the number of spaces indicated on the die and turns in one pack of supplies to the pot.

5. Follow the instructions along the sides for each space you land on. At spaces with no instructions you may, **but do not have to**, pick an Adventure Card depending on how adventurous you are. It could be good or bad!

6. At the finish (Montreal) you may trade your remaining goods and supplies for furs at the following value:
1 box of trade goods=1 bundle of furs
2 packs of supplies=1 bundle of furs.

7. If you run out of supplies, you may trade a pack from the pot or another player for a box of trade goods or a bundle of furs.

WAY

Thief River

RED

Rainy Lake River track

by the way of small brooks

Cowean

LAKE
WINEPEGOS

Leaf
Lake

RN

Mo river

carryroynr Meadow River

Trent River

Leech River

MISSISSIPPI RIVE

Swan River

H.L.

64

CHAPTER 8 *Star Gazer*

David Thompson

Most of us grow up with the help of our parents or guardians; but others, like little David Thompson, become orphans and are raised in institutions. The only home that David knew was the strict Grey Coast School in England; his father had died when David was a baby.

When the Hudson's Bay Company offered to pay the school 15 dollars for bright young apprentices, only David and one other student passed the tests. The other orphan heard that they were going to be sent to the cold, frozen northwest territories of Rupert's Land, and ran away from the school.

In 1784, 14-year-old David Thompson arrived at Churchill Factory, an outpost on Hudson Bay. He was short for his age, dark bangs of hair hung down to his eyebrows and he had been blind in his right eye since birth. This frail youngster would become one of the legends of the fur trade, a man the Indians would one day call "Stargazer."

His first job was to copy the manuscript of Samuel Hearne, a geographer and surveyor. As he transcribed Hearne's account of his journey to the Coppermine River, three-metre-high (10-foot) snowdrifts piled up within the walls of the stockade. However, a burning ambition inside his small frame grew and kept David warm. It was not an ambition for fame or wealth, but rather the desire to explore, to discover rivers, lakes and mountain passes and to place them on a map of the new continent for future generations.

When his outfit of clothing, which was supplied by the Hudson's Bay

Company, arrived from England, he turned it down and asked instead for a brass sextant. It would allow him to "shoot" the stars and determine the positions of lakes, rivers and trading posts.

Thompson was motivated by scientific curiosity. He studied surveying, learned to use a telescope, chronometer, compass, thermometer and, of course, his sextant. At 16 he became a writer and clerk for a trader, Mitchell Oman, in the western interior. Next he was sent to winter with the Piegan Indians on the shores of the Bow River (near Calgary). The following winter he was confined with a broken leg at Manchester House, a post on the north branch of the Saskatchewan River. In 1791, he was promoted to "Trader and Surveyor" and put in charge of his own expedition.

Thompson was earning a legendary reputation in the northwest as a colourful storyteller. He refused to drink rum or trade it to the Indians. Around the campfires on the cold trails, he would read from the Bible and give long sermons to his men. Although they were in competition, a

close friendship grew between Thompson and Nor'Wester Simon Fraser, who convinced David to leave the Hudson's Bay Company.

With the Hudson's Bay Company he had surveyed over 5,000 km (3,100 mi.) of rivers and lakes; with the North West Company he struggled on foot, in canoes, with snowshoes, and on horseback over 80,000 km (50,000 mi.) of rough terrain, recording 3,500,000 km (2,200,000 mi.) before he retired.

It was not his friend Simon Fraser, but David Thompson who finally found and traced the mighty Columbia River to the ocean. The day they started that journey, in 1811, he and his wife Charlotte along with three of their young children knelt to pray. "May God in His mercy give me to see where its waters flow into the ocean, and return in safety."

After 28 years in the northwest, Thompson retired to Montreal where, using his diary, he drew the first real map of the northwest. It was hung at Fort William for all northmen to use as a guide. David Thompson, one of history's best geographers, had fulfilled his dream.

Making Maps

Map makers like David Thompson took careful notes and kept journals of their travels. When they returned home they prepared maps for other travellers based on the information they had compiled. You can do the same!

What You Need:
small note book
pencil
tape measure
compass
large sheet of paper — 1/2 metre square (one and 1/2 ft.)

What To Do:

1. Before starting your journey, determine the length of your pace. Make a mark on the ground and take ten normal steps. Mark the spot where you stop and measure the distance with the tape measure. Divide the distance by ten. How long is your average pace? 1/2 metre?

2. Now begin your journey. Take a walk in your neighbourhood or a nearby park. Determine the direction you are walking with the compass and record it and the numbers of paces you are walking in that direction in your notebook. Be very careful crossing streets. Also note the things you see along the way — houses, streams, fences, trees, bridges. When you change direction, note that change in your notes.

3. When you return home transfer the information from your notebook onto the large sheet of paper to create your map. Each time you do this your maps will become more accurate. Now you can really appreciate David Thompson's accomplishments!

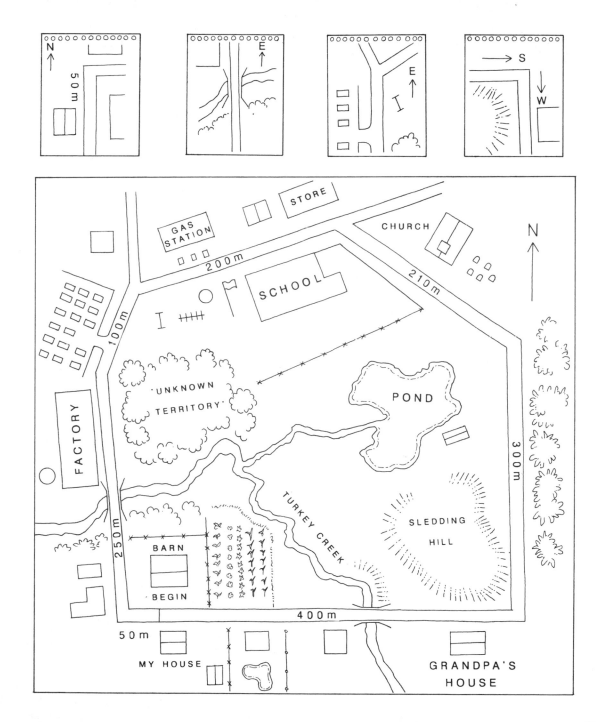

69

NATIVE TRIBES OF THE NORTHWEST

9 *Native People of the Northwest*

Indians and Inuit

Today Canada is known as a multicultural country. People come from a variety of racial backgrounds and speak many different languages in their homes. However, we are united by a common allegiance to the country of Canada and most of us speak English, although French is also an official language.

In the days before the fur traders, North America was a land of many nations and cultures, speaking more than 300 languages. The native tribes could not easily understand each other so they communicated with sign language and gestures. They had no written language, so they cut signs in the bark of trees, painted stories of historic events or kept a symbolic record in forms such as totem poles.

Subarctic Tribes

It was these natives who the fur traders relied on most to teach them to survive in the forests and to gather the beaver pelts. They lived in the northern land area called *taiga*, which includes a maze of inland waterways such as: Great Bear Lake, Great Slave Lake, Lake Winnipeg, Yukon River, Mackenzie River, Peace River, Saskatchewan River, and Red River.

These subarctic tribes did not live in permanent villages. They were always on the move, ready to follow the herds of deer or antelope which they hunted. Because they did not want to have too many things to carry, they had few possessions. They travelled in bands of 25 to 35 which were usually related by blood or marriage. The words for mother and aunt, or brother and male cousin, were the same in their language.

They travelled in birch-bark canoes or on snowshoes and wore fringed, buckskin clothing. The women liked to braid their hair and decorate it with colourful bands of shell or stone jewellery. The men went bareheaded to show off their long hair. The most respected man in the band was the best hunter.

Because of the harsh life and deadly diseases, babies frequently died. For this reason, a baby was not named when it was born, but after it became strong enough to live. Both girls and boys married at a very young age — a girl when she was able to have babies and a boy when he proved to be a hunter. The first time a young boy killed a wild animal was an important event.

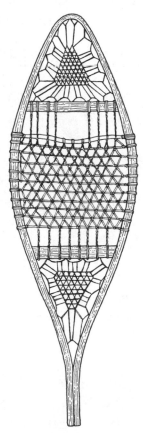

Kutchin Indians

It was Alexander Mackenzie who first entered the territory of the Kutchin Indians on his trip to the Arctic in 1789.

Carrier Indians

This tribe got its name from their custom of widows carrying the charred bones of their dead husbands in a basket for three years.

Chipewyan Indians

The name Chipewyan means "pointed skin" because Chipewyans' shirts were pointed at the bottom. When Samuel Hearne explored the Churchill, Coppermine and Slave rivers from 1768 to 1776, he was led by a Chipewyan guide named Matonabbee.

Indians of the Great Plains

These Indians were the best horsemen in the world. They depended on the buffalo herds, which they followed across the flat prairies, for food and clothing. They lived in portable tepees and used dogs and horses to drag *travois*, on which they carried all their possessions.

Shamans

The Inuit, the subarctic, the plains and the west coast Indians all had powerful *shamans* or medicine men. These were the elders in the tribes who had close contact with the spirit world.

Vision Quest

Before reaching puberty, a young girl or boy went on a "vision quest." They had to go alone and without food into the forest, and stay there until they met with a wild animal who would be their protector and friend. Using dreams to get in touch with the animal, they learned to respect it. Through this magical experience, they gained power and understanding of the animals they would hunt and depend on for food and clothing.

Sioux Sun Dance

The sun dance was performed in a sacred lodge to honour the sun, sky and earth. It was performed to keep the buffalo plentiful, to heal the sick, to make good marriages and to bring victory in battle. Sometimes the Indians would tear pieces of skin from their bodies to create the magic.

Gros Ventre Indians

Gros Ventre means "big belly" and was given to this tribe who were known as big eaters.

Assiniboine Indians

The name Assiniboine means "those who cook with stones."

Piegan Indians

Piegan, or *Pikuni*, means "poorly dressed."

Travois
This consisted of two poles tied together in a V shape. The closed end was placed on the shoulders of the animal and the open end was pulled behind on the ground. The wooden frame could double as tepee poles when plains Indians made camp.

Blood Indians
These Indians got their name because they painted their bodies with red clay.

Blackfoot Indians
The Blackfoot got their name from their custom of dyeing their moccasins black. A boy going on his first war party would be given a silly or insulting name until he stole his first horse or killed his first enemy. Then he would be given his real name based on his actions and behaviour.

People of the Northwest Coast

The coastal natives of British Columbia built their wooden houses on the sandy beaches facing the sea. Because they lived beside coastal forests of gigantic evergreens, they had become expert woodworkers. Their long cedar-plank houses varied in size from six to 30 metres (20 to 100 ft.) and often had giant totem poles in front of them. They made masks, hats and armour of wood. The sea provided them with food, including salmon, halibut, herring, cod, and flounder as well as seals, sea lions, and whales.

Potlatch

The potlatch was an Indian custom that varied in different tribes. It came from the Nootka word, *pat-shatl*, which means "sharing." It involved the giving of gifts to others to show your wealth and power.

Slave Killers

In the Kwakiutl version of the *potlatch*, the person receiving the gift had to repay with twice as much at the next potlatch ceremony. The gifts might be furs, blankets, cedar chests, copper plates or even slaves. Sometimes, the slaves were killed with a ceremonial club called a "slave killer" as a symbolic gift.

Talking Blankets

The name Tsimshian means "people of the Skeena River" and they were known for their beautiful woodwork and basketry. The animal and abstract designs woven from goat's hair and cedar bark on their fringed Chilkat blankets and shirts were supposed to have the power to talk to people.

Kidnapped by Wolves

Nootka boys had to undergo an initiation ordeal where they were kidnapped for days by men disguised as wolves. They learned wolf songs and dances before they were rescued in a mock battle.

Kwakiutl Masks

The Kwakiutl tribe carved and painted beautiful masks to which they added feathers and hair. They used the masks to tell stories about the spirits in their mythology. Some were used in the Cannibal Dance, a story about the Cannibal Spirit acted out to warn people against the evil of cannibalism.

Indian Bead Work

Originally the Plains Indians decorated their costumes with fringe, elks' teeth, ermine skins and dyed porcupine quills. After the arrival of the Europeans, the Indians acquired trade beads. These were then considered a more valued item for decorating clothing, bags and other items than the natural materials. Most of the Indian designs were geometric. You can make your own beads!

What You Need:
small plastic straws
scissors
thread
needle

What To Do:

1. Cut the plastic straws into different lengths to create your own beads.

straws

cut straws to desired lengths

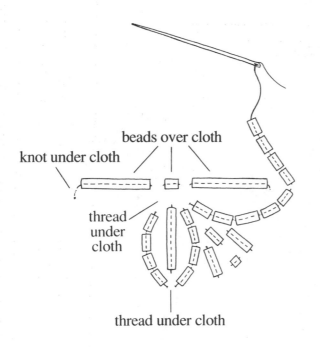

beads over cloth

knot under cloth

thread under cloth

thread under cloth

2. Bead work on cloth:

To begin, run the threaded needle through the back of the cloth (don't forget to tie a knot in the end of your thread). Next, string a bead and lay it over the top of the cloth. Then bring your needle through the top of the cloth to the back then back up through the top again. Repeat this process to complete your design.

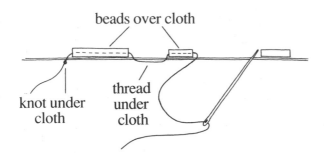

beads over cloth

knot under cloth

thread under cloth

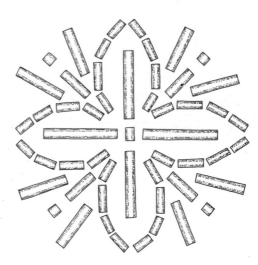

This is a completed Indian bead-work pattern. You may wish to create your own design.

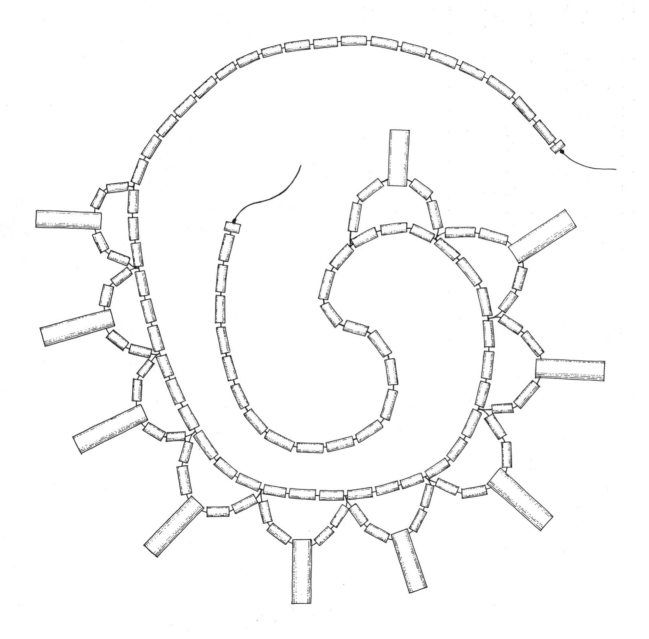

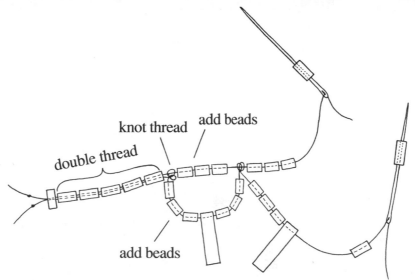

double thread · knot thread · add beads

add beads

3. **Bead-work necklace:** To make a necklace start with two different needles and thread. With the first length of thread make a continuous string of beads. To create a loop use the second needle and thread and run it through the same strand. Tie a knot with the second thread at the desired length and add more beads. Continue in this fashion until you finish. Don't forget to count your beads — it will make a nicer pattern.

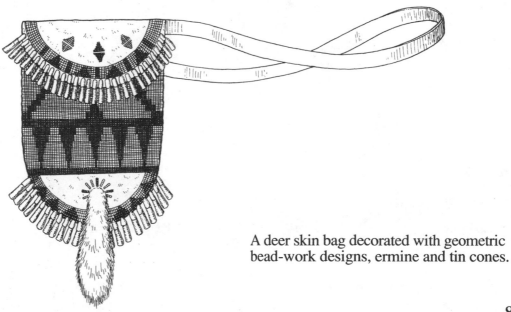

A deer skin bag decorated with geometric bead-work designs, ermine and tin cones.

10

Massacre At Seven Oaks

Lord Selkirk

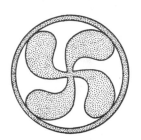

When the trader-merchants of Montreal joined forces and created the North West Company, they became a powerful force in the fur trade. The Nor'Westers ignored the Hudson's Bay Company which claimed to control all the trading in the northwest.

But the giant Hudson's Bay Company finally woke up and prepared to defend its territory and trade. A young Scottish earl, Lord Selkirk, created a Hudson's Bay Company settlement on the Red River beside the Nor'Westers' Fort Gibralter. He shipped thousands of emigrants from Scotland to Hudson Bay, then down the Nelson River to Lake Winnipeg.

The Nor'Westers feared the new settlement on their direct fur route to the northwest. The Métis resented the new settlers to whom the Hudson's Bay Company had granted 18 million hectares (45 million acres) of land.

The Highland Scots were rugged people, but the settlement was not well planned and many died of cold and hunger during the first winter. The Red River settlement became desperate for food. Miles MacDonnell, whom Selkirk had put in charge, seized 600 bags of pemmican from the Nor'Westers' Brandon Post on the Assiniboine River.

When the news reached Fort William, a Nor'Wester, Duncan Cameron, rushed to the Red River. He offered the settlers food only if they would leave the area and go to Montreal. The Métis attacked and burnt down the home of a settler who refused to go, so over 100 accepted Cameron's offer.

When Lord Selkirk heard the news, he immediately sent a new governor to the colony — a strong-minded military captain, Robert Semple. Semple arrested Duncan Cameron and sent him to England to stand trial for his actions. Then he tore down the Nor'Westers' Fort Gibralter log by log.

Led by Cuthbert Grant, an angry mob of Métis and Nor'Westers rode on horseback to the Hudson's Bay Company's fort near Seven Oaks. Robert Semple went out to meet them, arrogantly demanding to know what they wanted. "We want our fort!" screamed Grant. "Then go to your fort!" taunted Semple as he grabbed for the bridle of Grant's horse. A shot rang out and Semple fell dead. Semple's men rushed from the fort. Firing broke out everywhere. Men shot at each other from behind trees or on horseback. When the fighting was over, 20 of Semple's men had died with him and the others were shipped to Fort William as prisoners. Only one Nor'Wester died at Seven Oaks; the others celebrated their victory.

However, the party was a short one. Lord Selkirk came from Scotland to Montreal, had himself appointed a justice of the peace for Canada, hired a private army of 100 Swiss mercenaries and, along with hundreds of *voyageurs* from Upper Canada, set out for Fort William.

An awesome brigade of canoes charged swiftly across Thunder Bay and up to the gates of Fort William. The Scottish earl demanded the release of the prisoners taken at Seven Oaks. He arrested William McGillivray, the head of the North West Company, and all the partners in the fort, then sent them to Montreal for trial.

The years that followed were filled with clashes between Nor'Westers and Hudson's Bay Company employees. Forts were seized on both sides, brigades of canoes were ambushed at portages and men were murdered throughout the northwest. Finally, in 1821, the two rival companies agreed to join together under the Hudson's Bay Company, and the last of the beaver wars was over.

Sasquatch Footprints

On January 5, 1811, while travelling to Athabasca, David Thompson recorded in his journal the local natives' belief in a huge "mammoth" which could have been the creature we now call a *sasquatch:*

I questioned several; none could positively say they had seen him, but their belief I found firm and not to be shaken.

Two days later, he wrote:

In the afternoon, we came on the track of a large animal. I measured it; four large toes each of four inches (10 cm) *in length, to each a short claw; the ball of the foot sunk three inches* (seven cm) *lower than the toes, the hinder part of the foot did not mark well; the length, fourteen inches by eight inches* (35 by 20 cm) *in breadth; walking from north to south and having passed about six hours. The men and Indians would have it to be a young mammoth, and I held it to be the track of a large old grizzly bear; yet the shortness of the nails, the ball of the foot, and its very great size was not that of a bear.*

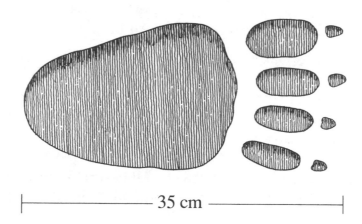

|— 35 cm —|

Northwest Crossword Puzzle

ACROSS:

4. An Indian medicine man

5. Food used by fur traders

7. Used by plains Indians to carry heavy loads

8. A Nor'Wester who shot the rapids

9. A tribe in which young boys were kidnapped by men disguised as wolves

11. French-Canadian canoe men

16. The canoe used on the Great Lakes

19. An instrument used by early explorers to calculate their positions

20. A beaver's house

21. The explorer who made the first map of the northwest

DOWN:

1. The first explorer to reach the Rocky Mountains

2. The man who created the Red River settlement

3. The man whose vision created the Hudson's Bay Company

6. The bosses of the fur trade

10. The highways used by the fur traders

12. A mythological monster who lives in the Rocky Mountains

13. An emergency canoe, used when speed was important

14. An Indian custom that involved sharing gifts

15. A tribe in which a boy, on his first war party, was given a silly or insulting name

16. The first explorer to cross the North American continent

17. The canoe used in the far northwest

18. People who are half-white and half-Indian

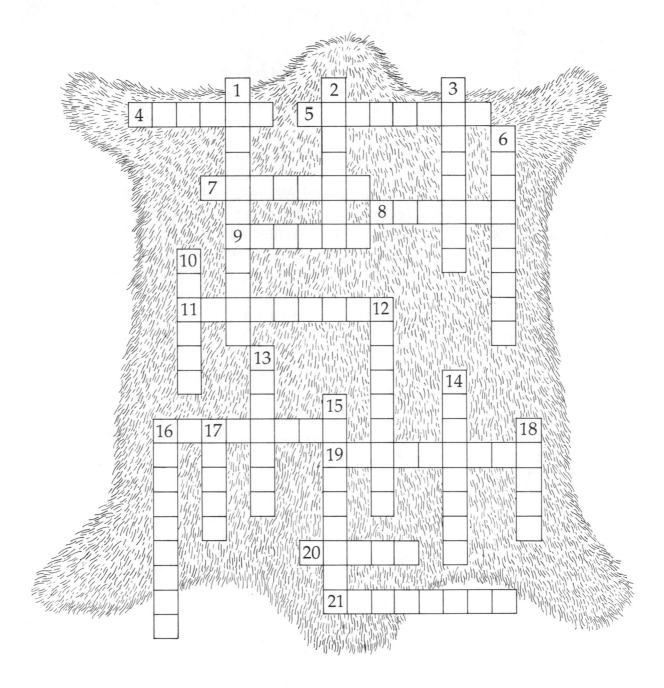

CHAPTER 11

Friends to the Rescue

Grey Owl and Anahareo

Today, fur trapping employs thousands of Canadians. The monopoly of the Hudson's Bay Company no longer exists, but the hunters in the northern regions of Canada still do. One of them who lived in this century, a trapper named Grey Owl, was destined to become as famous as the Nor'Westers.

The story really began in England where a young boy named Archie Belaney was raised by his two elderly aunts. He had never known his parents.

One of the great joys in Archie's life was his books about the wild west of North America. Stories of the frontiersmen and Indians had always fascinated and thrilled him. So in 1906, when he turned 16, he left school and sailed to Canada. He worked in Toronto only long enough to save the money for the train fare to Cobalt in northern Ontario.

The train tracks were washed out, so the passengers had to walk the last 65 km (40 mi.). Archie was hungry and without money. His British accent made him a target for ridicule; he was badly beaten in a fight. Bitten by insects and weak from hunger, he lost consciousness beside the tracks and swarms of black flies settled on his face.

"Lucky we came across you when we did, or you'd be food for the wolves by now." As Archie's eyes blinked open, he saw the dark, weather-beaten face of Jesse Hood, a professional guide. He had woken up in a log cabin and behind Jesse stood two silent Indians.

Thus began a new life for Archie. He learned to canoe, snowshoe, trap, to go dog-sledding, and to speak the Ojibway language. As his complexion darkened from the outdoor life, his English accent faded. Dressed in his buckskin clothing, he looked like his Indian friends. He was adopted into the Ojibway tribe and named *Wa-Sha-Quon-Asin* or Grey Owl.

Everyone had accepted him as an Indian by the time he met and married a beautiful Indian woman named Anahareo. Her quiet and sensitive nature grew on him. She hated to see beaver and other wild animals killed and mutilated in ugly steel traps.

"You must stop this work," she urged; "It is killing your spirit as well as mine."

They adopted two small beaver cubs, the first of many wild pets, whose parents had been killed by trappers and Grey Owl, the conservationist, was born. As the baby beavers nuzzled under his chin and curled up on his chest to sleep, Grey Owl realized the cruelty of trapping wild animals. Thanks to Anahareo, he would no longer hunt animals for a living.

"I am now the president, treasurer, and sole member of the Society of the Beaver People," he declared.

Grey Owl began writing and speaking about the slaughter of the beaver. Dressed as a Canadian Indian, he became a world-famous celebrity. His articles in magazines, his books on wildlife and his lecture tours made people in Europe and North America aware of the inhumane massacre taking place in the wilderness. With the help of the Canadian National Parks Service, he set up a conservation reserve for the beavers.

But when Grey Owl died of pneumonia on April 13, 1938, at Prince Albert, Saskatchewan, the newspaper headlines read: "Grey Owl a Fraud."

The world was shocked to learn that the famous Canadian Indian conservationist was not an Indian at all, but a white man from England named Archie Belaney. Even his wife Anahareo had never guessed the truth.

Answers to Northwest Crossword Puzzle, page 86

ACROSS

4. *shaman*
5. pemmican
7. *travois*
8. Fraser
9. Nootka
11. *voyageurs*
16. Montreal
19. astrolabe
20. lodge
21. Thompson

DOWN

1. LaVérendrye
2. Selkirk
3. Radisson
6. *bourgeois*
10. rivers
12. sasquatch
13. Express
14. *potlatch*
15. Blackfoot
16. Mackenzie
17. North
18. Métis

Index